PIANO • VOCAL • GUITAR

SONGS OF THE '90

THE DECADE SERIES

ISBN 0-7935-6667-3

HAL•LEONARD®
CORPORATION
7777 W. BLUEMOUND RD. P.O. BOX 13819 MILWAUKEE, WI 53213

SONGS OF THE '90s

THE DECADE SERIES

- *Laptop Computers*

- *Pagers*

- *Dream Teams*

OPRAH WINFREY REMAINED QUEEN OF DAYTIME TV.

THE NINETIES

THE 90s

BY ELAINE SCHMIDT

As Americans careened toward the twenty-first century, they did so with cell phones ringing, pagers beeping, palm pilots glowing and lap-tops humming. All this while multi-tasking at a furious pace. As the nineties unfolded, technology invaded every corner of private and business life. Millions began to telecommute from home, keeping in constant touch with the office through phone, fax and Internet connections. Executives took conference call meetings on golf courses, while soccer moms ordered carry-out dinners while piloting kid-filled minivans.

Crammed into these hectic lives was a near frantic concern with fitness. From Tae-Bo classes to sure-fire diets that ranged from no-fat to no-carbohydrates, Americans obsessed about weight whether or not they lost it. Living longer and retiring earlier than ever before, aging Americans sent *Modern Maturity* to the #1 spot on magazine subscription charts. As members of the much-ballyhooed Baby Boom generation started turning fifty in 1995, their children, dubbed Generation X, searched to find an identity separate from that of their parents. In fashion, a retro craze rendered a second generation of young people victims of seventies styles, while their parents relaxed into "working-casual" mode of dress.

A decade of superlatives, the nineties saw the advent of superstores, Dream Teams, the enormous Mall of America, and the information superhighway. From the Wonderbra in the world of lingerie and "great rooms" in home design, to the mutation of the television set into high-definition, big-screen, surround-sound home theater, no area of American life was safe from the quest for grandeur.

Like all previous decades of the twentieth century, the American nineties have come to be defined by a few key events and trends. In sports, a baseball strike canceled a World Series game, Michael Jordan's first retirement from basketball, a closely-watched home run race and the appearance of young golf phenomenon Tiger Woods were in the headlines. The bombing of the Murrah federal building in

Oklahoma and the first bombing of the World Trade Center left indelible images in many minds. The country mourned with the Kennedy family when Jacqueline Kennedy Onassis died in 1994 and again when John F. Kennedy Jr. and his wife Carolyn Bessette Kennedy and her sister died in a plane crash. The entire world mourned when Princess Diana was killed in a Paris car crash in 1999.

Green became a concept, as environmental awareness increased. Green spaces brought grass and trees back to urban areas. Green designs created environmentally-friendly buildings and homes, while green products were touted as being non-toxic and biodegradable. The terms global warming and greenhouse effect moved into the national vocabulary as we donned high SPF sunscreen to protect ourselves from the ever-widening hole in the ozone layer.

Entertainment took on new dimensions in the nineties. Lines between entertainment and news were obscured as 24-hour cable news and sports channels searched the world for stories to fill air time. Print news thrived in national news magazines like *Newsweek*, *Time* and *U.S. News and World Report*, while the immediacy of television news took a predictably heavy toll on local newspapers. Many papers took their wares to the Internet, struggling to remain relevant in the technology age.

Entertainment and politics also merged as Bill Clinton, the first member of the Baby Boom generation to be elected president, hit the presidential campaign trail with saxophone in hand. Throughout the decade politicians lapped up air time anywhere they could find it, from talk show appearances during the campaigns to sitcom and endorsement appearances by the likes of Bob Dole following his defeat in the presidential race. Radio talk jock Rush Limbaugh further blurred the lines between politics and entertainment, bringing his self-

proclaimed political expertise to the airwaves, while Bill Maher argued virtually anything via the televised "Politically Incorrect." All this while late night parodies of political figures took on lives of their own.

Politics and scandal walked through the decade hand-in-hand. The Clinton administration was plagued by allegations and investigations, making Whitewater, Kenneth Starr and Paula Jones household names. Political scandal hit its apex as the story of President Clinton's involvement with a young White House intern named Monica Lewinsky unfolded. His unsuccessful impeachment and the constant barrage of details from the relationship left most Americans hoping for a return to the more mundane business of politics.

On the home front, the Internet invaded American homes following the early nineties debut of the World Wide Web. Terms like e-commerce, SPAM and FAQs worked their way into everyday speech. Americans soon began shopping from online stores and auction sites, while discount online travel services put travel agents at risk of obsolescence. Private lives too were affected, through cyber-dating romances to chat-room friendships.

Video Cassettes were replaced by DVDs, while writeable CDs replaced cassette tapes. Cars grew in size, with minivans and sport utility vehicles replacing the family car. Starbucks gave us designer coffee while Einsteins and the like gave us designer bagels. The Macarena had the nation dancing, while Martha Stewart became the empress of homemaker wisdom, and Feng Shui determined living room layouts. Among the decade's fads were in-line skates, Beanie Babies, Furby, Tickle Me Elmo, and yo-yos. Virtually anything could be sold by infomercial.

In Hollywood, studios scrambled to find the next mega-hit. History seemed a hot topic for films with *Apollo 13*, *Saving Private Ryan* and *Titanic* serving up the past. Audiences feasted on Jane Austen's *Sense and Sensibility*, wept over Steven Spielberg's *Schindler's List*, and embraced revisionist history through *Dances With Wolves*. Yet

budget did not seem to be a factor in determining success. Dismal responses to the big-budgeted *Waterworld* and *Cliffhanger* shook studio confidence, while the offbeat *Forrest Gump* hit the $300 million dollar mark at the box office and became a cultural touchstone along the way. *The Blair Witch Project* cost almost nothing to make but made millions. Another low-budget independent film, *Smoke Signals*, opened in art houses, quietly shifting to mainstream theaters as its audience grew. Stars of the decade included Tom Hanks, who could do no wrong, Tom Cruise, and "America's Sweetheart," Julia Roberts, who managed to match male stars in her per-film salary.

And then there were children's movies. The biggest box office hit of 1995 was Disney's *The Lion King*, but the receipts were only the beginning of the story. Like many other successful family films, it hit additional pay dirt with the sale of everything from coloring books to children's clothing and bed linens. Elton John wrote the music for the film's songs and rode the wave of popularity with his recording of "Can You Feel the Love Tonight."

Once upon a time, Hollywood looked to Broadway for movie ideas. During the nineties a cautious Broadway turned its eyes to Hollywood for supposedly proven ideas, bringing Disney to the Great White Way with *The Lion King* and *Beauty and the Beast*. Broadway's financial conservatism brought a host of revivals to the stage, including *Show Boat*, *Carousel*, *Guys and Dolls*, and *How to Succeed in Business Without Really Trying*. Andrew Lloyd Webber remained a bankable name in the business with multiple companies of *The Phantom of the Opera* and *Cats* on tour, and *Sunset Boulevard* a hit on stage.

Television too adopted a split personality in the nineties, waffling between breaking new ground and following tried-and-true formats with others. When "Roseanne" worked, "Grace Under Fire" followed. "Seinfeld" worked, so "Friends," "Mad About You" and bevy of other chummy, urban sitcoms capitalized. "Beverly Hills 90210" begat "Melrose Place," which then begat a chic parade of up-scale, prime time soaps. The animated "Simpsons" defied successful copying. Kelsey Grammar continued the "Cheers" legacy with his witty, urbane spin-off "Frasier." But not all shows followed predictable patterns. "The X-Files" popularized paranoia while "N.Y.P.D. Blue" pushed the network limits of language and nudity.

Sexual orientation became a central topic in "Ellen" and "Will and Grace." "Seinfeld" was the benchmark of television success, making "anti-dentites," Festivus, and "closer-talkers" part of the American vernacular. Oprah remained the reigning royalty of the talk show world, while Jerry Springer redefined strident confrontation and Rosie O'Donnell reacted with a gentle-spirited talk show of her own.

Fashion, ranging from grunge to glam and hip-hop to preppie, was an anything goes proposition for most of the decade. While designer names like Liz Claiborne and DKNY soared in popularity, the younger generation wore oversized pants perched precariously low on their hips. Microfiber and tencel fabrics appeared, giving a fresh unrumpled look to men's and women's fashion. Meanwhile, body piercing and tattoos, better known as body art, contributed to a somewhat different look.

The publishing industry spent the decade reaching for the proverbial brass ring. Writers wishing to publish literary fiction were most often sent packing, while O.J. Simpson, his legal team and jurors, and nearly anyone who has ever laid eyes on the British royal family received red carpet treatment. Nonfiction dominated the book market, from cookbooks to aftermarket software manuals and ... *for Dummies* and *The Idiot's Guide to...* (insert virtually anything here). Oprah's book club had millions rushing to purchase her latest recommendation. Project Gutenberg put entire books online while the publishing industry mistakenly predicted a great publishing revolution in the form of the e-book.

On the consumer front, bookstores went through swift, striking changes. In 1990 a book-seeker would likely have headed to a local bookshop or a chain bookstore in a shopping mall for a quick look around and a purchase. By mid-decade the book superstore had invaded most American cities, transforming browsing into a lengthy adventure in through recordings, periodicals, newspapers, software, stationery, greeting cards, and, oh yes, books. All this while sipping a latté from the on-site coffee shop.

There was a time when it was easy to define styles within the realm of popular music. People's tastes were fairly predictable by age and race. Not so in the nineties, where rap, the music of black, urban youth had its biggest sales among white, suburban teens and country superstars found their biggest audiences in large urban centers. If there was a trend in the nineties, it was the lack of a unified trend.

LAPTOP COMPUTERS BECAME AN ICON OF THE ERA.

A look at the Grammy Awards for the decade tells the whole story. Oldsters Tony Bennett, Santana and Eric Clapton and Bob Dylan were Album of the Year winners, as were relative youngster Celine Dion and newcomer Lauryn Hill. The Billboard charts tell the same story of diversity. Elton John and Puff Daddy were on the Billboard Top 10 list in 1998. Cher and Britney Spears were there in 1999. The Backstreet Boys shared the 1998 Billboard Top Album list with Garth Brooks, while Barbra Streisand and the Notorious B.I.G. were both on the Top Album charts in 1997.

This individual freedom in pop music and specialized radio formats meant that the striking stylized sounds of Mariah Carey ("Hero," "Vision of Love"), Luther Vandross ("Here and Now"), and Boyz II Men ("End of the Road," "In the Still of the Nite") shared the pop charts with 900-year-old Gregorian chant that

inexplicably wandered over from the classical charts. Jon Bon Jovi roared to success with "Blaze of Glory," from the movie *Young Guns II*, and showed his mellower side with his namesake band in "Always." Tony Bennett found a new generation of fans with his renditions of standards, while pop fixture James Taylor showed remarkable staying power with a 1997 Grammy for best Pop Album (*Hourglass*). Feeling disenfranchised by society in general and pop music in particular, Generation X-ers turned to the folk-rock sounds of former frat band Hootie and the Blowfish, putting "Hold My Hand" on the charts along with Ace of Base's "The Sign," and "All That She Wants," R.E.M.'s "Losing My Religion" and EMF's "I Believe."

Crossover artists have had a field day with pop diversity. Garth Brooks scored a huge hit with "Friends in Low Places," and sold tens of millions of albums. For a while, Billy Ray Cyrus's "Achy Breaky Heart" was everywhere. At the same time "The Three Tenors" – classical singers Jose Carreras, Placido Domingo and Luciano Pavarotti – garnered huge success in recordings, videos, concerts, and books. They toured the world, bringing live classical music to throngs of adoring fans. Their first album sold twelve million copies worldwide. Their success spawned several other tenor trios, including Three Irish Tenors, Three Celtic Tenors, and Three Mo' Tenors, an African-American triumvirate.

Duets enjoyed a resurgence in popularity, perhaps led by Frank Sinatra's collaborations with a variety of pop music's hot properties. Celine Dion teamed with Clive Griffin to resurrect the standard "When I Fall In Love" for the movie *Sleepless in Seattle*, and joined Peabo Bryson to record the title track for Disney's *Beauty and the Beast*. Bryson changed partners for the follow-up hit, singing "A Whole New World" from *Aladdin*, with Regina Belle. Linda Ronstadt and Aaron Neville blended voices for the tender "Don't Know Much." Meanwhile Bryan Adams, Rod Stewart and Sting were heard as a trio in "All for Love" the theme song for – what else? – *The Three Musketeers*.

Reunion tours and "best of" boxed sets continued to generate income for classic rock groups. Even the Beatles made a comeback in 1995 and '96, via "new release" anthology albums and an extended television documentary. Baby Boomers defiantly held on to their favorite pop stars until a younger

generation finally discovered them, extending the careers of the now middle-aged rockers to multiple decades. Eric Clapton started an acoustic trend with his 1992 *Unplugged* album. Elton John racked up hits with Disney, redid his 1974 single "Don't Let the Sun Go Down on Me" with George Michael, and took his "Candle in the Wind" back onto the charts as a eulogy for his friend, Princess Diana. Meat Loaf staged a revival of his one-album career with "I'd Do Anything for Love (But I Won't Do That)."

But perhaps more newsworthy than the music itself was the way consumers listened to it. Writeable CDs and MP3 technology, combined with an illicit online service known as Napster, allowed music lovers to copy tunes from the Internet for no fee for a time. Napster was a

CAL RIPKEN, JR. BECAME A SPORTS LEGEND BY BREAKING LOU GEHRIG'S MAJOR LEAGUE RECORD OF CONSECUTIVE GAMES PLAYED.

huge loss of revenues for record labels as well as losses of royalties for recording artists and songwriters. Though eventually shut down by the courts, the recording industry had seen the possible future and hastily shifted gears in response.

As the decade ended, and the much-anticipated year 2000 arrived, Americans stockpiled canned goods and waited for the Y2K bug to bring society to its knees. (It didn't, if you haven't heard.) The decade had left the Soviet Union disintegrated and the Middle East ready to ignite. The votes were still out as to whether the World Wide Web was drawing citizens of the world closer together or isolating them in front of their computers. We learned to fear terrorism and crime in the

MICHAEL JORDAN ACHIEVED LEGENDARY STATUS IN THE NBA.

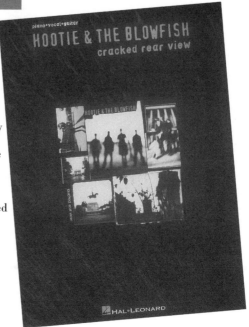

nineties, and were sold security systems for our homes, cars and computers. Even personal alarms had their day in the sun. But we also enjoyed greater freedom to work and travel as we pleased, defining our own lifestyles in ways previous generations could not have imagined. American life changed radically over the course of the past century, the most dramatic changes occurring since World War II. Whether they were the best of times or the worst of times, they were our times, with diversity and personal freedom not previously experienced in the history of the world.

STATISTICS

STATISTICS

1989–1990 SEASON

OUTSTANDING DRAMA SERIES: "L.A. LAW"

OUTSTANDING COMEDY SERIES: "MURPHY BROWN"

1990–1991 SEASON

OUTSTANDING DRAMA SERIES: "L.A. LAW"

OUTSTANDING COMEDY SERIES: "CHEERS"

1991–1992 SEASON

OUTSTANDING DRAMA SERIES: "NORTHERN EXPOSURE"

OUTSTANDING COMEDY SERIES: "MURPHY BROWN"

1992–1993 SEASON

OUTSTANDING DRAMA SERIES: "PICKET FENCES"

OUTSTANDING COMEDY SERIES: "SEINFELD"

1993–1994 SEASON

OUTSTANDING DRAMA SERIES: "PICKET FENCES"

OUTSTANDING COMEDY SERIES: "FRASIER"

1994–1995 SEASON

OUTSTANDING DRAMA SERIES: "NYPD BLUE"

OUTSTANDING COMEDY SERIES: "FRASIER"

1995–1996 SEASON

OUTSTANDING DRAMA SERIES: "ER"

OUTSTANDING COMEDY SERIES: "FRASIER"

1996–1997 SEASON

OUTSTANDING DRAMA SERIES: "LAW AND ORDER"

OUTSTANDING COMEDY SERIES: "FRASIER"

1997–1998 SEASON

OUTSTANDING DRAMA SERIES: "THE PRACTICE"

OUTSTANDING COMEDY SERIES: "FRASIER"

1998–1999 SEASON

OUTSTANDING DRAMA SERIES: "THE PRACTICE"

OUTSTANDING COMEDY SERIES: "ALLY MCBEAL"

SUPERBOWLS

1990 San Francisco over Denver

1991 New York over Buffalo

1992 Washington over Buffalo

1993 Dallas over Buffalo

1994 Dallas over Buffalo

1995 San Francisco over San Diego

1996 Dallas over Pittsburgh

1997 Green Bay over New England

1998 Denver over Green Bay

1999 Denver over Atlanta

WORLD SERIES

1990 Cincinnati over Oakland

1991 Minnesota over Atlanta

1992 Toronto over Atlanta

1993 Toronto over Philadelphia

1994 No World Series due to players' strike

1995 Atlanta over Cleveland

1996 New York over Atlanta

1997 Florida over Cleveland

1998 New York over San Diego

1999 New York over Atlanta

THE NINETIES

ACHY BREAKY HEART
(DON'T TELL MY HEART)

Words and Music by
DON VON TRESS

You can tell the world you
You can tell your ma I

nev-er was my girl. ___
moved to Ark-an-sas. ___

You can burn my clothes when I'm
You can tell your dog to bite my

gone.
leg.

Or you can tell your friends ___ just
Or tell your broth-er Cliff ___ whose

might blow_ up and kill this man. Ooh. _____

man.

All For Love

from Walt Disney Pictures' THE THREE MUSKETEERS

Words and Music by BRYAN ADAMS,
ROBERT JOHN "MUTT" LANGE and MICHAEL KAMEN

When it's love you give ___ (I'll be a man of good
___ (I swear I'll al-ways be
___ (I'll be the fire in your

faith.) then in love you'll live. ___ (I'll make a stand. I won't break.)
strong.) then there's a rea-son why. ___ (I'll prove to you we be-long.)
night.) then it's love you take. ___ (I will de-fend, I will fight.)

I'll be the rock you can build on, ___
I'll be the wall that pro-tects you ___
I'll be there when you need me. ___

ALL THAT SHE WANTS

Words and Music by buddha, joker,
jenny and linn

She leads a lone - ly__ life.__ She leads a lone - ly__ life.__

Well she woke up late in the morn-ing light and the

ALWAYS

Words and Music by
JON BON JOVI

Slow rock ballad

This Ro - me - o is bleed - ing,
pic - tures that you left be - hind are just

Well, there ain't no luck __ in these

BABY BABY

Words and Music by AMY GRANT
and KEITH THOMAS

BEAUTIFUL IN MY EYES

Words and Music by
JOSHUA KADISON

Colors of the Wind
from Walt Disney's POCAHONTAS

Music by ALAN MENKEN
Lyrics by STEPHEN SCHWARTZ

BEAUTY AND THE BEAST

from Walt Disney's BEAUTY AND THE BEAST

Lyrics by HOWARD ASHMAN
Music by ALAN MENKEN

Can You Feel The Love Tonight

from Walt Disney Pictures' THE LION KING

Music by ELTON JOHN
Lyrics by TIM RICE

DON'T KNOW MUCH

Words and Music by BARRY MANN,
CYNTHIA WEIL and TOM SNOW

END OF THE ROAD

Words and Music by BABYFACE,
L.A. REID and DARYL SIMMONS

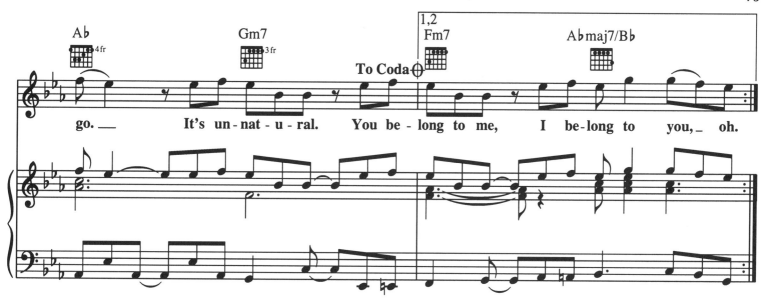

go. ___ It's un-nat-u-ral. You be-long to me, I be-long to you, ___ oh.

long to me, I be-long to you. Al-though we've

long to me, I be-long to you. ___

Additional lyrics

(*Spoken:*) *Girl, I'm here for you.*
   All those times at night when you just hurt me,
   And just ran out with that other fellow,
   Baby, I knew about it.
   I just didn't care.
   You just don't understand how much I love you, do you?
   I'm here for you.
   I'm not out to go out there and cheat all night just like you did, baby.
   But that's alright, huh, I love you anyway.
   And I'm still gonna be here for you 'til my dyin' day, baby.
   Right now, I'm just in so much pain, baby.
   'Cause you just won't come back to me, will you?
   Just come back to me.

   Yes, baby, my heart is lonely.
   My heart hurts, baby, yes, I feel pain too.
   Baby please...

FOREVER IN LOVE

By KENNY G

FORREST GUMP - MAIN TITLE
(FEATHER THEME)
from the Paramount Motion Picture FORREST GUMP

Music by
ALAN SILVESTRI

Sweetly

THEME FROM "FRASIER"

from the Paramount Television Series FRASIER

Words by DARRYL PHINNESSEE
Music by BRUCE MILLER

FRIENDS IN LOW PLACES

Words and Music by DEWAYNE BLACKWELL
and EARL BUD LEE

HAVE I TOLD YOU LATELY

Words and Music by
VAN MORRISON

HOLD MY HAND

Words and Music by DARIUS CARLOS RUCKER, EVERETT DEAN FELBER,
MARK WILLIAM BRYAN and JAMES GEORGE SONEFELD

HERE AND NOW

Words and Music by TERRY STEELE
and DAVID ELLIOT

HERO

Words and Music by MARIAH CAREY
and WALTER AFANASIEFF

HOW AM I SUPPOSED TO LIVE WITHOUT YOU

Words and Music by MICHAEL BOLTON
and DOUG JAMES

I DON'T HAVE THE HEART

Words and Music by ALLAN RICH
and JUD FRIEDMAN

MCA music publishing

I'D DO ANYTHING FOR LOVE
(BUT I WON'T DO THAT)

Words and Music by
JIM STEINMAN

I BELIEVE

Words and Music by JEFFREY PENCE,
ELIOT SLOAN and EMOSIA

Walk blind - ly to ____ the light ___ and reach out for ___ his hand.
Vi - o - lence has spread ___ world wide and there's fam - 'lies on ___ the street.
I've been see - ing Lis - a now for a lit - tle o - ver a year.

love will find _ a way. _____

D.S. al Coda

I'LL MAKE LOVE TO YOU

Words and Music by
BABYFACE

Close your eyes, make a wish, and blow
lax, let's go slow. I ain't

IN THE STILL OF THE NITE
(I'LL REMEMBER)

Words and Music by
FRED PARRIS

LOSING MY RELIGION

Words and Music by BILL BERRY, PETER BUCK,
MIKE MILLS, MICHAEL STIPE

OPPOSITES ATTRACT

Words and Music by
OLIVER LEIBER

Additional Lyrics

4. She's got the money, and he's always broke.
   I don't like cigarettes, and I like to smoke.
   Things in common, just ain't a one.
   But when we get together we have nothin' but fun.

5. Baby, ain't it somethin' how we lasted this long?
   You and me provin' everyone wrong.
   Don't think we'll ever get our differences patched.
   Don't really matter 'cause we're perfectly matched.

ONE SWEET DAY

Words and Music by MARIAH CAREY, WALTER AFANASIEFF, SHAWN STOCKMAN,
MICHAEL McCARY, NATHAN MORRIS and WANYA MORRIS

THE POWER OF LOVE

Words by MARY SUSAN APPLEGATE and JENNIFER RUSH
Music by CANDY DEROUGE and GUNTHER MENDE

Save the Best for Last

Words and Music by PHIL GALDSTON,
JON LIND and WENDY WALDMAN

THEME FROM "SCHINDLER'S LIST"

from the Universal Motion Picture SCHINDLER'S LIST

Composed by
JOHN WILLIAMS

THE SIGN

Words and Music by buddha, joker,
jenny and linn

Reggae pop

(I,) I got a new _ life. You'd hard-ly rec-og - nize_ me. I'm_ so glad.
(I,) un-der the pale _ moon for so man - y years I won-dered who_ you are.

TEARS IN HEAVEN

Words and Music by ERIC CLAPTON
and WILL JENNINGS

Would you know my name _____
Would you hold my hand _____
Would you know my name _____

if I saw you in heav - en?
if I saw you in heav - en?
if I saw you in heav - en?

Would it be the same _____
Would you help me stand _____
Would you be the same _____

Be - yond   the   door ___   there's peace,   I'm   sure. _

THE RIVER OF DREAMS

Words and Music by
BILLY JOEL

blind, _____ in the mid-dle of the night. _____

dreams, _____ in the mid-dle of the

VISION OF LOVE

Words and Music by MARIAH CAREY
and BEN MARGULIES

WHEN I FALL IN LOVE

Featured in the TriStar Motion Picture SLEEPLESS IN SEATTLE

Words by EDWARD HEYMAN
Music by VICTOR YOUNG

A WHOLE NEW WORLD
(ALADDIN'S THEME)
from Walt Disney's ALADDIN

Music by ALAN MENKEN
Lyrics by TIM RICE

WITH ONE LOOK
from SUNSET BOULEVARD

Music by ANDREW LLOYD WEBBER
Lyrics by DON BLACK and CHRISTOPHER HAMPTON,
with contributions by AMY POWERS

NORMA With one look I can break your heart, with one look I play ev - ery part.

I can make your sad heart sing, with one look you'll know all you need to know.

With one smile I'm the girl next door or the love that you've hun - gered for.

WIND OF CHANGE

Words and Music by
KLAUS MEINE

Whistle

I fol - low the Mos - kva ___ down to Gor - ky Park ___
The world is clos - ing in. ___ Did you ev - er think
Walk - ing down the street, ___ dis - tant mem - o - ries ___

like a storm-wind that will ring___ the free-dom bell ___ for peace of mind.__

Let ___ your ba - la - lai - ka sing___ what my gui - tar ____ wants to sing.__

in the wind of change.

Whistle

THE DECADE SERIES

The Decade Series explores the music of the 1890s to the 1980s through each era's major events and personalities.
Each volume features text and photos and over 40 of the decade's top songs, showing how music has acted as a
mirror or a catalyst for current events and trends. All books are arranged for piano, voice and guitar.

Songs Of The 1890's
55 songs, including: Asleep In The Deep • Hello! Ma Baby • Maple Leaf Rag • My Wild Irish Rose • 'O Sole Mio • The Sidewalks Of New York • Stars And Stripes Forever • Ta Ra Ra Boom De Ay • When You Were Sweet Sixteen • and more.
00311655 ....$12.95

Songs Of The 1900's – 1900-1909
57 favorites, including: By The Light Of The Silvery Moon • Fascination • Give My Regards To Broadway • Glow Worm • Meet Me In St. Louis • Take Me Out To The Ball Game • Yankee Doodle Boy • and more.
00311656 ....$12.95

Songs Of The 1910's
57 classics, including: After You've Gone • Ah! Sweet Mystery Of Life • Danny Boy • Let Me Call You Sweetheart • My Melancholy Baby • Oh, You Beautiful Doll • When Irish Eyes Are Smiling • You Made Me Love You (I Didn't Want To Do It) • and more.
00311657 ....$12.95

Songs Of The 20's
58 songs, featuring: Ain't Misbehavin' • April Showers • Baby Face • California Here I Come • Five Foot Two, Eyes Of Blue • I Can't Give You Anything But Love • Manhattan • Stardust • The Varsity Drag • Who's Sorry Now.
00361122 ....$14.95

Songs Of The 30's
61 songs, featuring: All Of Me • The Continental • I Can't Get Started • I'm Getting Sentimental Over You • In The Mood • The Lady Is A Tramp • Love Letters In The Sand • My Funny Valentine • Smoke Gets In Your Eyes • What A Diff'rence A Day Made.
00361123 ....$14.95

Songs Of The 40's
61 songs, featuring: God Bless The Child • How High The Moon • The Last Time I Saw Paris • Moonlight In Vermont • A Nightingale Sang In Berkeley Square • A String Of Pearls • Swinging On A Star • Tuxedo Junction • You'll Never Walk Alone.
00361124 ....$14.95

Songs Of The 50's
59 songs, featuring: Blue Suede Shoes • Blue Velvet • Here's That Rainy Day • Love Me Tender • Misty • Rock Around The Clock • Satin Doll • Tammy • Three Coins In The Fountain • Young At Heart.
00361125 ....$14.95

Songs Of The 60's
60 songs, featuring: By The Time I Get To Phoenix • California Dreamin' • Can't Help Falling In Love • Downtown • Green Green Grass Of Home • Happy Together • I Want To Hold Your Hand • Love Is Blue • More • Strangers In The Night.
00361126 ....$14.95

Songs Of The 70's
More than 45 songs including: Don't Cry For Me Argentina • Feelings • The First Time Ever I Saw Your Face • How Deep Is Your Love • Imagine • Let It Be • Me And Bobby McGee • Piano Man • Send In The Clowns • You Don't Bring Me Flowers • You Needed Me.
00361127 ....$14.95

Songs Of The 80's
Over 40 of this decade's biggest hits, including: Candle In The Wind • Don't Worry, Be Happy • Ebony And Ivory • Endless Love • Every Breath You Take • Flashdance...What A Feeling • Islands In The Stream • Kokomo • Memory • Sailing • Somewhere Out There • We Built This City • What's Love Got To Do With It • With Or Without You.
00490275 ....$14.95

MORE SONGS OF THE DECADE SERIES

Due to popular demand, we are pleased to present these new collections with even more great songs from the 1920s through 1980s. Each book features beautiful piano/vocal/guitar arrangements. Perfect for practicing musicians, educators, collectors, and music hobbyists.

More Songs Of The 20's
Over 50 songs, including: Ain't We Got Fun? • Bill • Carolina In The Morning • Fascinating Rhythm • The Hawaiian Wedding Song • Malagueña • Nobody Knows You When You're Down And Out • Someone To Watch Over Me • Yes, Sir, That's My Baby • and more.
00311647 ....$14.95

More Songs of the 30's
Over 50 songs, including: All The Things You Are • A Fine Romance • In A Sentimental Mood • Just A Gigolo • Let's Call The Whole Thing Off • Mad Dogs And Englishmen • Stompin' At The Savoy • Stormy Weather • Thanks For The Memory • and more.
00311648 ....$14.95

More Songs Of The 40's
Over 60 songs, including: Bali Ha'i • Be Careful, It's My Heart • Five Guys Named Moe • The Last Time I Saw Paris • Old Devil Moon • San Antonio Rose • Some Enchanted Evening • Too Darn Hot • and more.
00311649 ....$14.95

More Songs Of The 50's
56 songs, including: Blueberry Hill • Chanson D'Amour • Charlie Brown • Do-Re-Mi • Hey, Good Lookin' • Hound Dog • I Could Have Danced All Night • Mack The Knife • Mona Lisa • My Favorite Things • (Let Me Be Your) Teddy Bear • That's Amore • and more.
00311650 ....$14.95

FOR MORE INFORMATION, SEE YOUR LOCAL MUSIC DEALER, OR WRITE TO:

HAL•LEONARD™
CORPORATION
7777 W. BLUEMOUND RD. P.O. BOX 13819 MILWAUKEE, WI 53213

Prices, contents, and availability subject to change without notice
Some products may not be available outside the U.S.A.

More Songs Of The 60's
66 songs, including: Alfie • Baby Elephant Walk • Bonanza • Born To Be Wild • Eleanor Rigby • Moon River • Raindrops Keep Fallin' On My Head • Seasons In The Sun • Sweet Caroline • Tell Laura I Love Her • What The World Needs Now • Wooly Bully • and more.
00311651 ....$14.95

More Songs Of The 70's
Over 50 songs, including: Afternoon Delight • All By Myself • American Pie • Billy, Don't Be A Hero • Happy Days • Honesty • I Shot The Sheriff • Maggie May • Maybe I'm Amazed • She Believes In Me • She's Always A Woman • Wishing You Were Here • and more.
00311652 ....$14.95

More Songs Of The 80's
43 songs, including: Addicted To Love • Call Me • Don't Know Much • Footloose • Girls Just Want To Have Fun • The Heat Is On • Karma Chameleon • Longer • Straight Up • Take My Breath Away • Tell Her About It • We're In This Love Together • and more.
00311653 ....$14.95

STILL MORE SONGS OF THE DECADE SERIES

What could be better than even *more* songs from your favorite decade! These books feature piano/vocal/guitar arrangements with no duplication with *earlier volumes*.

Still More Songs Of The 30's
Over 50 songs including: April in Paris • Body And Soul • Heat Wave • It Don't Mean A Thing (If It Ain't Got That Swing) • and more.
00310027 ....$14.95

Still More Songs Of The 40's
Over 50 songs including: Any Place I Hang My Hat • Don't Get Around Much Anymore • If I Loved You • Sentimental Journey • and more.
00310028 ....$14.95

Still More Songs Of The 50's
Over 50 songs including: Autumn Leaves • Chantilly Lace • If I Were A Bell • Luck Be A Lady • The Man That Got Away • Venus • and more.
00310029 ....$14.95

Still More Songs Of The 60's
Over 50 more songs, including: Do You Know The Way To San Jose • Duke Of Earl • Hey Jude • I'm Henry VIII, I Am • Leader Of The Pack • (You Make Me Feel) Like A Natural Woman • What A Wonderful World • and more.
00311680 ....$14.95

Still More Songs Of The 70's
Over 60 hits, including: Cat's In The Cradle • Nadia's Theme • Philadelphia Freedom • The Way We Were • You've Got A Friend • and more.
00311683 ....$14.95

0395

Contemporary Classics

Your favorite songs for piano, voice and guitar.

The Definitive Rock 'n' Roll Collection

A classic collection of the best songs from the early rock 'n' roll years – 1955-1966. 97 songs, including: Barbara Ann • Chantilly Lace • Dream Lover • Duke Of Earl • Earth Angel • Great Balls Of Fire • Louie, Louie • Rock Around The Clock • Ruby Baby • Runaway • (Seven Little Girls) Sitting In The Back Seat • Stay • Surfin' U.S.A. • Wild Thing • Woolly Bully • and more.

00490195..$24.95

The Big Book Of Rock

78 of rock's biggest hits, including: Addicted To Love • American Pie • Born To Be Wild • Cold As Ice • Dust In The Wind • Free Bird • Goodbye Yellow Brick Road • Groovin' • Hey Jude • I Love Rock N Roll • Lay Down Sally • Layla • Livin' On A Prayer • Louie Louie • Maggie May • Me And Bobby McGee • Monday, Monday • Owner Of A Lonely Heart • Shout • Walk This Way • We Didn't Start The Fire • You Really Got Me • and more.

00311566...$19.95

Big Book Of Movie And TV Themes

Over 90 familiar themes, including: Alfred Hitchcock Theme • Beauty And The Beast • Candle On The Water • Theme From *E.T.* • Endless Love • Hawaii Five-O • I Love Lucy • Theme From *Jaws* • Jetsons • Major Dad Theme • The Masterpiece • Mickey Mouse March • The Munsters Theme • Theme From *Murder, She Wrote* • Mystery • Somewhere Out There • Unchained Melody • Won't You Be My Neighbor • and more!

00311582 ....$19.95

The Best Rock Songs Ever

70 of the best rock songs from yesterday and today, including: All Day And All Of The Night • All Shook Up • Ballroom Blitz • Bennie And The Jets • Blue Suede Shoes • Born To Be Wild • Boys Are Back In Town • Every Breath You Take • Faith • Free Bird • Hey Jude • I Still Haven't Found What I'm Looking For • Livin' On A Prayer • Lola • Louie Louie • Maggie May • Money • (She's) Some Kind Of Wonderful • Takin' Care Of Business • Walk This Way • We Didn't Start The Fire • We Got The Beat • Wild Thing • more!

00490424 ....$16.95

The Best Of 90s Rock

30 songs, including: Alive • I'd Do Anything For Love (But I Won't Do That) • Livin' On The Edge • Losing My Religion • Two Princes • Walking On Broken Glass • Wind Of Change • and more.

00311668 ....$14.95

35 Classic Hits

35 contemporary favorites, including: Beauty And The Beast • Dust In The Wind • Just The Way You Are • Moon River • The River Of Dreams • Somewhere Out There • Tears In Heaven • When I Fall In Love • A Whole New World (Aladdin's Theme) • and more.

00311654...$12.95

55 Contemporary Standards

55 favorites, including: Alfie • Beauty And The Beast • Can't Help Falling In Love • Candle In The Wind • Have I Told You Lately • How Am I Supposed To Live Without You • Memory • The River Of Dreams • Sea Of Love • Tears In Heaven • Up Where We Belong • When I Fall In Love • and more.

00311670...$15.95

The New Grammy® Awards Song Of The Year Songbook

Every song named Grammy Awards' "Song Of The Year" from 1958 to 1988. 28 songs, featuring: Volare • Moon River • The Shadow Of Your Smile • Up, Up and Away • Bridge Over Troubled Water • You've Got A Friend • Killing Me Softly With His Song • The Way We Were • You Light Up My Life • Evergreen • Sailing • Bette Davis Eyes • We Are The World • That's What Friends Are For • Somewhere Out There • Don't Worry, Be Happy.

00359932 ....$12.95

Soft Rock – Revised

39 romantic mellow hits, including: Beauty And The Beast • Don't Know Much • Save The Best For Last • Vision Of Love • Just Once • Dust In The Wind • Just The Way You Are • Your Song.

00311596 ....$14.95

37 Super Hits Of The Superstars

37 big hits by today's most popular artists, including Billy Joel, Amy Grant, Elton John, Rod Stewart, Mariah Carey, Wilson Phillips, Paula Abdul and many more. Songs include: Addicted To Love • Baby Baby • Endless Love • Here And Now • Hold On • Lost In Your Eyes • Love Takes Time • Vision Of Love • We Didn't Start The Fire.

00311539 ....$14.95

Prices, contents & availability subject to change without notice.